Your Essential Guide to Achieving Success in Any Job Interview

Table of Contents

Introduction

Sooner or later, everyone must face the daunting task of interviewing for a job. Whether it's for just a job to keep your bills paid, or if it's the dream job you've always wanted, there are many things that you have to remember before you can get that job that you so desire.

Most people assume that the most important part of a job interview is showing up well groomed, but there is more to it than that. Everything that you could ever want may be riding on your behavior at a job interview. The smallest thing can mean the difference between your having a new job, or you're still pounding the pavement trying to score a new interview.

It is common knowledge that it is generally the smallest detail that causes people to fail a job interview. The fact that you can score an interview at all shows that you already have the right stuff for the job. However, scoring the interview is merely the first step in the journey that is to get you the job of your dreams.

This book is to be your comprehensive guide to winning that job that you so crave. In following the steps listed here, you will have all of the knowledge required to get your body through that door that you are most trying to step into. In this book, you will learn:

- How to get the interview of your choice.

- How to prepare for the interview.

- How to make a great first impression.

- How to conduct yourself during the interview.

- What the most common questions are.

- What questions to ask your interviewer.

- What common mistakes you should avoid making.

- About the post interview follow-up.

- Questions that interviewers cannot ask.

Chapter 1

How to Get the Interview

Scoring the interview for the job that you want doesn't have to be rocket science. Sometimes you can score that interview by simply making a phone call. There are many ways that people go about trying to get an interview. The methods of achieving one vary by company. It is best to know what the company's application process is before taking your first step.

Generally, when a company is hiring they post an ad in the newspaper or an online job bank. How to contact them is usually included in the ad as well. You don't want to email a resume to a company that is requesting that you walk in with your resume. You don't want to call a company that requires a faxed resume etc. Ignoring their initial contacting information will guarantee that you will not get that interview because you have already proven that you can't follow simple directions.

Sometimes, you can get a job lead from a friend before the job has been posted. If this is the case, you can either ask the friend to give the employer your resume and cover letter. If your friend doesn't actually work where the lead came from, you can try calling about the position and ask what the application procedure is.

There are four general methods of applying for a job, and they include these basic methods.

Sending a Resume

Some companies prefer that you mail in your resume. For this type of approach, it is best to include a cover letter with your resume. The cover is a basic letter that describes the position that you are interest in and a few details of your qualifications and skills. It is basically your lead in to your resume. Before writing your cover letter, you should know whom the letter is to be addressed to. You never want to begin a cover letter with "Dear Sir or Madame" or "To whom it may Concern". It shows that you have not prepared, and that you are not looking for a specific position with their company, but any job that you can get your hands on. Basically, it is disrespectful to your prospective employer.

Emailing Your Resume

Emailing resumes is becoming a commonplace way for recruiters to get resumes. Most companies offer this method as an alternative to the others. However, there are few tips on how you should go about it.

You should attach your resume as a word document or PDF file. These are the most common formats and what most companies will accept. The subject line should read like this: Smith, John (clerical position). This makes it easy for the recruiter to know who the email is from, and what it pertains to. It also assures that your email will be read.

Sometimes there are specific methods for addressing an emailed resume. Some companies have certain subject line requirements so follow them. If your company wants you to paste your resume, don't send attachments because your email will be deleted right away.

Faxing Your Resume

Again, you will need to include a cover letter when you fax in your resume. If you are not using your own fax machine, be sure to include your proper contact information. The rules for your cover letter are the same as for mailing your resume. More about cover letters will be provided a bit later on in this book.

Walk-In Your Resume

For this type of application procedure, you will want to dress appropriately. You would want to dress just like you would for an interview. Company's usually ask you to do this if you are going to be working directly with customers. They ask for a walk in because they want to get a look at your grooming habits right away. Sometimes, a walk in will have the employer giving you a brief interview on the spot, to see if they will require a formal interview later. So be on your best and most appropriate behavior.

Also, walk-ins do not require you to bring in a cover letter with your resume. Your appearance is sort of the cover letter. Sometimes, you will be requested to fill out an application form as well. Smile and be polite, no matter who you are talking to. That could be the difference between getting an interview and just taking an extra trip for nothing.

Telephoning for an Interview

It is not particularly common anymore for companies to ask you to call them for an interview. That is usually saved for jobs that include sales and/or jobs that are not so easily applied for by the other methods. Telephoning for an interview is a bit common when a company requires that you be on the phone a lot. It gives them a feel for the quality and the personality of the person on the phone. When making this type of interview request, always speak in a clean and clear manner. Be polite and prepared to answer any questions that may be asked of you. You might approach the telephone interview like this:

"Hello Mr. Brown, I am Mike Sandal. I am calling with regards to your ad in the Post about the clerical position". If you are asked your experience and/or previous work experience, be prepared to answer quickly and explain how long you have been doing that type of work and give a brief description of your duties.

The correct way to build your resume will be included later on in this manual. It will give you the correct way to format your resume so that it gets noticed for all of the right things.

Preparing for the Interview

Once you get the call for the interview, the next thing that you have to do is prepare for it. You can never over prepare for an interview. The more prepared you are, the harder it will be to make mistakes. It is best to prepare yourself emotionally as well as intellectually for an interview. Giving a great interview is not as hard as some may think, but not as easy as others do either. Here are a few things that must be done in order to prepare for your next interview.

Remember, during an interview, you are a salesman. You are there to sell yourself to your prospective employer. You want to market yourself in the most interesting way possible. Great preparation for the interview is your best bet. A salesman that is knowledgeable, friendly and positive always gets the close.

Do Your Research

It doesn't matter how much knowledge or experience you have about the position that you are trying to get in a company if you don't have a clue who the company is or what they do. It is disastrous to enter into an interview and not be able to tell your interviewer what their company is about. How else are you going to tell them why you feel that you would be a good addition to their company?

A good and less time consuming way to get to know about a company is to look up their website. You can get all of the general knowledge about them that way, including the names of key people and their job titles. (There will be more on that in a minute) You should sift through most of their pages, including the pages that show samples of their work and/or products.

You can also look them up in the media files if there are any. Read the articles about them and soak in as much information as possible. Another thing that would be nice to do is to check out the surrounding area around the company. It makes for a nice breaker during the interview. You can make a comment about a particular monument or resting place nearby.

A trickier way to get a little extra information about the company is to call them on the phone and ask general questions, without referring to yourself as a potential employee. It's a nice way to get the goods on upcoming promotions etc.

Know Your Contact

When called for an interview, ask to whom you will be talking to. It is nice to be able to greet your interviewer by name at the beginning of the interview without first being told who they are. It shows that you are on top of things, and have prepared before hand.

You will also want to do some research on the person that will be conducting your interview. Learn what they do for the company and try to get some samples of their work or achievements in the company.

If you know what department that you are going to work in you may want to get the names of your potential colleagues and superiors prior to the interview as well. This way you can get some information about their roles in the company and the types of work that they have done.

Mention some of the things that you learn about your potential colleagues in the interview and about how much you look forward to working with them in the future. If you can, give an example of their work so that you will appear more sincere.

Practice Your Responses

It is best, if you are prone to nervousness, to practice giving your responses to the questions that may be asked of you. (A list of the most common questions will appear later on in the manual) You should practice your wording and the tone of voice that you plan to use; Try keeping your responses as brief as possible, but with as much detail as you can.

When you are trying to work out the proper responses to the interviewer's questions, you will also want to practice the art of getting your nerves under control as well as ridding yourself of any other odd habits while talking; like expressing yourself with your hands.

Practice answering your interview questions with a friend. Get his or her opinion about your delivery and gestures. Perhaps your friend will have some nice insights for you to use during the real interview.

Dress the Part

Pre-select your attire the day before your interview. You want to make sure that your clothes do not have any wrinkles or stains on them. Pick an outfit that best suits the type of job that you are applying for. If you are going to work in an office setting, you should dress conservatively. Soft earth tones are best for women. Try to avoid miniskirts and shirts that show too much skin. A nice dark suit is good for a male.

Of course if you are planning to work outdoors or in an artistic environment, you can dress a little more casually. Just be certain to avoid wearing denim jeans, over sized clothing, and under sized clothing. Women should try and avoid wearing too much make-up as well. It gives the wrong impression.

Even in the hotter seasons, you should not wear sandals or gym shoes to an interview. It sends an unprofessional message. The same goes for hats and other accessories.

Get Organized

Make sure that all of the things that you will need for the interview are prepared the day before. Make a checklist of the things that you will need if you have to. You should always have an extra resume handy during the interview. You should also bring with you a note pad to take notes during the interview if needed. (Only write down the important things that you think you will need to remember)If you have a business card, have one handy, it makes for easy contact later, and it also shows that you are professional and may help the employer to remember your name.

Chapter 2

How Should I Act?

There are many things that you can do that can take some of the pressure off during an interview. The way that you behave is one of the most important. It's not all in the words that come out of your mouth, but often has a lot to do with the mannerisms that you use.

Interviewers are not just wondering if you are skilled enough for the job, they are often wondering if you would fit in nicely with you co-workers. Your personality is a big part of your interview and can make all the difference. Here are some of the little things that you should pay particularly close attention to during an interview.

You do not want to be chewing gum or breath mints during your interview. You also don't want to speak in slang during your interview either. It is unprofessional and rude.

Show Confidence

You cannot enter into an interview with a defeatist attitude. You cannot mope or exude too much placidity in your manner. It is not inviting, and does not give the impression of a person that you want to face every day.

Be sure of your abilities without appearing cocky or narcissistic. You want to let you interviewer know that you are equipped to perform well at your job, without alienating other workers. You should point out your accomplishments in your field while remaining somewhat humble.

List your accomplishments in a matter of fact way without going into too much detail. I know this sounds repetitive, but you can never get this point too strongly. Understand that body language plays a large part in exuding confidence to others. Sit straight. Practice good posture, and keep your head up.

Keep a Positive Attitude

You should always try to smile and keep a positive outlook during your interview. If what you are hearing something that doesn't sound good to you, don't frown and look disgruntled, just keep a slight smile on your face until it is time for you to say something. Then approach your interviewer with your questions or concerns when the time is appropriate.

Maintain Eye Contact

Keeping eye contact with your interviewer is very important, especially when one of you is speaking to the other. If you are looking around the room or at the items on the interviewer's desk, you will appear uninterested. Just imagine what you would be thinking if you were speaking to him and he was looking all over the room. You would probably think that you already lost the interview.

Body Language

We've touched on this a little bit but you should mind some of the common errors that many people make when they are speaking to others. I've listed some of the common things that you should avoid when sitting through an interview.

- Avoid fidgeting while speaking to your interviewer. It shows a lack of self confidence.

- Avoid speaking while using overly expressive hand gestures. It is distracting.

- Avoid biting your lips in between sentences. It gives the impression that you are making things up.

- Do not sit with your arms crossed because it makes you appear stand-offish.

- Do not shrug your shoulders when asked a question that you are unsure of. Take a second to think of your response. Shrugging your shoulders gives the impression that you don't know the answer.

- Don't answer with nods and head shakes. Use your words to answer questions.

- Get plenty of sleep the night before the interview. You don't want to yawn in front of the interviewer. He will think that you are expressing boredom.

Your First Impression

First impressions can be a hard thing to get past in any situation. During an interview you want to give the best first impression that you can. There are many small things that you can do to assure that you give the best impression possible. They are as follows:

- You can never be too polite to the person that directs to your waiting area when waiting to be interviewed. A small gesture like, asking how they are doing can work wonders for you when you leave the building later.

- While waiting to be interviewed, sit properly and behave as if everyone passing you by is your potential interviewer. (They just might be) Smile at people as much as possible. Do not act impatient or bored, it sends the wrong message. Some interviewers will keep you waiting just to see how you handle yourself.

- Greet you interviewer with a firm handshake and a smile.

- Remain standing until your interviewer asks you to be seated. It is simply polite and shows proper etiquette.

- Again, dress according to the type of job that you are applying for.

- Show yourself to be well organized, by having all things needed for the interview.

- While waiting do not eat or drink anything.

- Don't chat on your cell phone while waiting for your interviewer. It makes you look distracted.

Your Resume

This may seem like an unimportant thing during an interview, but this is the sole reason why you may get that interview so you should be prepared with a well written resume.

You should tailor your resume to highlight the qualifications, work experience and any education that you've had that best represents the type of work you are applying for. You should also include any other work experience that you've had, as well as any accomplishments that you have made in your field.

You may also want to dress up your resume to let it stand out a bit. A nice border is an elegant way to make your resume stand out without being a distraction to the information within it.

Of course there also quite a few things that recruiters hate to see on resumes as well. Many people do not think that recruiters really go all the way through a resume, but they really do. Recruiters have certain pet peeves when it comes to reading a resume. I've included a list of some of the pet peeves that you should avoid when putting your resume together. These are the things that recruiters hate to see.

- Hiding or not including vital information on a resume is like death. A recruiter needs to see all of your important information without having to search for it.

- Major gaps in your employment history leave a recruiter wondering about your work ethic. Be prepared to answer questions if you have such gaps in yours.

- Summaries that are hard to follow and understand are annoying to recruiters. Keep your summary easy and brief.

- Use easy and simple fonts. Fancy fonts and colors are not eye catching in the manner that you likely wanted it to be. Yours will become to how-to on making resume errors.

- Avoid writing your resume as a narrative or in the first or third person. It is really irritating for a recruiter, and comes off as arrogant and/or egotistical.

- Pictures and/or graphics on a resume is distracting to a recruiter. Things like that will likely get your resume tossed out without a glance.

- Needlessly adding objectives and introductions on your resume bores recruiters. They know what your objective is, and your resume is not meant to be a novel.

- Lying or putting misleading information on your resume is a major no-no. There are always ways for a recruiter to check up on you and many do, so don't lie. Getting caught in a lie on a resume just says that you can't be trusted.

- Adding unnecessary information on a resume like your hobbies is completely useless. You should save that section to describe any accomplishments that you have made in your field.

- Sending a resume that doesn't match the type of job that you are applying for is extremely irritating to a recruiter. You are wasting their time.

- Using overly long paragraphs in a resume will get yours tossed aside. It is harder for the recruiter to read and makes the task take too long.

- Resumes that are more than two pages will not be fully read by a recruiter. That's just the way it is.

- Dating the information in your work history in the wrong order makes your resume harder to follow. (Work history should be listed with most current jobs at the top)

- Resumes that have too much detail when talking about your previous duties are a waste of your time. Duties are generally just sifted through. They are rarely given very much attention, just enough to give the recruiter an idea of what you have done in the past.

- Spelling and grammatical errors just proves that you are not very keen on details.

Chapter 3

Dos and Don'ts

There are quite a few things that you should do and not do during an interview that could make the whole thing a lot easier for both you and the interviewer. I have listed them quickly in the table below.

Dos	Don'ts
Arrive on time, or better yet 10 minutes early.	Be overly aggressive or egotistical
Refer to the interviewer by name.	Spend too much time talking about money.
Smile and use a firm handshake.	Act uninterested in the company or the job.
Be alert and act interested throughout.	Act defensively when questioned about anything.
Maintain eye contact at all times.	Speak badly about past colleagues or employers.
Make all comments in a positive manner.	Answer with only yes or no.
Speak clearly, firmly, and with authority.	Excuse your bad points about work history.
Except any refreshment offered.	Excuse yourself halfway through the interview, even if you have to use the bathroom.
Promote your strengths.	Ask for coffee or refreshments.

Your Cover Letter

Creating the perfect cover letter does not have to be difficult. Cover letters are generally short and to the point. You should address your cover to someone in particular. You should never address your cover letter with "To whom it may Concern" or "Dear Sir/Madame" it is unprofessional and doesn't show a genuine interest in the company or the job.

The cover letter is the sole purpose for looking at the resume. If it is written badly, the resume might not get a once over. In most cases, the resume is just as important as the resume, so I have briefly written the right formation of one.

The cover letter should begin with a basic greeting and the position that you are applying for. It should be nor more than 2 lines long. The second paragraph should be a brief description of your qualifications and why you applied to work for them. The closing should announce an interest in hearing from them soon, and a thank you for their time. Here is a sample of a successful cover letter.

****

July 4, 2004

In regards to: The clerical position that is available.

Mr. Brown
3232 Jackson St.
Jackson City, FA
32443
Attention: Mr. Joe Brown

Dear Mr. Brown,

This letter is in regards to the clerical position that is recently available in your company. As my enclosed resume will show you, I have three years experience as a clerk.

During my career I have successfully integrated a new filing system for my previous employer, Wayne Law Firm that increased their productivity by 33%. That filing system is still in use there now, and has been integrated into two other companies.

I thank you for your time in reading this letter. I hope to hear from you once you have had time to read my resume.

Respectfully,

The Restaurant Interview

Sometimes recruiters will ask you to conduct your interview during lunch or dinner. It makes for a more relaxed setting for the recruiter, but you should remember that it is still an interview, and your behavior must be in accordance to that.

During this type of interview, you should try to look at it as a relaxing way for you to talk about and sell yourself to the recruiter. Making a little bit of small talk is expected. Do not bring up the topic of the interview until the interviewer does. He/she might want to get to know you a bit first.

Remember to talk about yourself, but do not get too personal. There are also basic points of etiquette and common sense rules that you should follow as well. They are as follows:

- Remember your basic table manners, like putting your elbows on the table etc.

- Always fold your napkin on your lap before eating.

- Do not order messy or sloppy foods. That includes finger foods like ribs, and extremely large sandwiches. Avoid pastas with thick sauces, and French fries.

- Do not order the most expensive item on the menu either.

- Avoid alcoholic beverages if you can.

- When you get up to use the restroom, place your napkin on your chair or on the arm of your chair.

- Common sense; don't smack your lips or talk with your mouth full.

- Always excuse yourself if you plan to leave the table for any reason.

- Do not have your cell phone turned on.

- Continue to speak formally to your interviewer unless requested not to.

After your interview is over, be certain to thank the recruiter for the meal and their time. Offer a firm handshake, and ask when you should expect to hear from them. It shows confidence and a continued interest in the job. Send a thank you card that same day.

Closing the Interview

Once you have run the bases of the interview, it is still important that you end the interview well. The hard part is over and now all that is left is for you close out the interview in the same winning manner.

Wait until your interviewer stands up or requests that you do. Give your closing greeting. Thank the interviewer for his taking the time to see you. Offer another firm handshake, and ask when you might know when you might expect to hear from them about their decision.

Extra Tips

With all of the information that was given in this manual, you would think that you have learned everything that there is to know about acing an interview. However there are still a few extra tips that you should know, and a few more helpful hints.

1. Market your skills and related experience in the field that you are applying for. Be sure to do it in a way that is positive and not cocky.

2. Researching the company before your interview is a good way to know where you would fit into it. It lets the employer know that you really want to be a part of the company too.

3. Bring your list of questions with you in a folder with the company's name on it with you so that you don't forget them. You should also keep your extra resumes in there too.

4. You want to describe your weaknesses as strengths. For example, saying that you are overenthusiastic about performing at your best.

5. Since many interviewers ask you what your biggest fault might be, you should pick a fault that is actually a good thing. Try saying "I don't take on projects that I can't give 110% on.

6. Let your interviewer bring up the topic of salary first.

7. Don't volunteer your personal opinions to your interviewer about any subjects unless you are asked.

8. Try to establish a good rapport with your interviewer. Be casual but professional, and most importantly BE YOURSELF!

Common Interview Questions

Every interview compiles of the interviewer asking you a great deal of questions. Many of them are standard questions that every interviewer asks. I've listed the most common questions that you will encounter during an interview to help you get a handle on them before you go to one. It is always good to be prepared.

By reading these common questions that interviewers ask, you will have a leg up on the competition. You will also have time to prepare your answers so that you don't get stumped. So here is your key to acing a job interview.

1. Tell me something about yourself. Remember, say something positive.

2. How do handle stressful situations?

3. How do you deal with criticism and stress?

4. What is your definition of success?

5. Why do you think that you would fit in with this company? (This is where your research comes in handy)

6. Have you ever been fired, and why?

7. Where do you see yourself in 5 years?

8. Do you prefer to work on your own or as a team?

9. Why are you interested in working for this company?

10. How do you handle a difference of opinion with your colleagues or superiors?

11. Why should I hire you?

Chapter 4

Common Questions when Applying for Your First Job After College Graduation

1. Tell me what your most rewarding college experience was.

2. What extracurricular activities did you participate in?

3. What have you learned in college that applies directly to this job?

4. How have you prepared yourself for the transition from college to the workplace?

5. Are you going to graduate school? If so, do you plan to continue working as well?

6. How do you plan to manage graduate school and working?

7. Did you get any hands on experience in College?

8. How do you feel that college has prepared you for this job?

9. Have you ever done an internship that helped to prepare you for this type of work?

10. What do you think is the best asset that you could bring to the company?

Questions That You Should Ask Your Interviewer

Just like you will be fielding questions from your interviewer, it is best to ask a few of your own. It shows that you are genuinely interested in working there, and that you have some concerns of your own. It also shows that you feel relatively certain that this is the place for you.

Asking the right questions to your prospective employer will show him/her that you are serious in you efforts to work for their company, and that you are an organized individual. You should steer clear of asking any personal questions or any questions that are not directly job related.

If you wish, you may jot down some of the answers that you are given for reference later on. Keep your questions simple and polite. Make sure that you are asking direct questions about the job and/or work environment.

Here are some questions that you should ask your prospective employer:

1. Why is this position available right now?

2. How many times has this position been filled in the past 5 years?

3. What should the new person do that is different from the last person that had this position?

4. What would you most like to see done in the next 6 months?

5. What are the most difficult problems that this jobs entails?

6. How much freedom do I have in the decision making process?

7. What are my options for advancement?

8. How has this company succeeded in the past?

9. What changes do you envision in near future for this company?

10. What do you think constitutes success in this job?

Questions Employers Cannot Ask

Just like there are many questions that an interviewer can ask, there are many that he cannot ask. Some questions are illegal to ask. Many people don't realize that there are off limit questions for employers. That is why I felt that it was important to include them.

When or if you do encounter some of these questions there are ways that you can choose to respond to them. Since some people would probably answer them, it is good to know that you don't have to answer those kinds of questions. You can simply ask how those questions pertain to the job you're applying for. Here is a list of the questions that are illegal for an interviewer to ask.

1. Questions about your age are not allowed during an interview because it should not be a factor upon hiring you.

2. Questions about your marital status are inappropriate and can easily be mistaken for sexual harassment. This question also applies to whether or not you have children, your child care plans etc. This type of question also includes any other aspect of your personal life that should not affect your chances of being hired.

3. Questions about your personal health are also off limits.

4. Questions about your ethnicity should not be asked by an interviewer or answered by the person being given the interview.

5. Your sexual preference cannot be a factor in your chances of being hired either. This type of question should not be asked.

6. Whether or not you have disabilities is a question that should not be asked either.

7. Your arrest record is information that doesn't have to be answered. All an interviewer can ask you is if you have ever been convicted of a crime, they cannot ask you what for or how many times.

8. Basically, personal information cannot be asked by an interviewer. It is illegal, and you do not have to respond.

The Post Interview Follow-up

Now that the interview is over, the hard work is over, but you still have to follow up on the interview later. Sending a thank you note is the best way to start. The thank you letter should be written with your thanks for their time and consideration in seeing you.

If you haven't heard from the employer within a week, you should call the office to ask if they have reached a decision yet. This is not being pushy; it shows your enthusiasm and persistence. If they haven't reached a decision, ask when you might expect to hear from them. If they don't give an answer try again in another week and so on.

What Employers Are Looking For

When an employer decides to conduct an interview with you, there are certain things that they are looking for from you. Naturally, you are likely to focus on these things during an interview, but you should remember all of the tips in this manual because following those tips is what is going to make the employers see all of those things in you.

Since everybody wants to have a leg up when it comes to an interview, it naturally seemed to be appropriate to let you in on what the employers are evaluating you on during an interview. So here is that list.

- Your Enthusiasm: **Employers want to know that you are willing and eager to be a part of their company. Being fully stocked with knowledge about the company is a sure fire way to show your enthusiasm.**

- Your ability to speak clearly: **If you approach an interview mumbling and speaking slang, a prospective employer will not see you as a professional.**

- Showing your teamwork skills: **You should show an example of your ability to work as a team during your interview.**

- Leadership skills: **You should show your leadership abilities by approaching your interview with an offensive train of thought.**

- Problem solving ability: **Employers needs to know that you can handle yourself when a problem arrives.**

- Work related experience: **You definitely want to show that you have some experience in the field already, so that the employer knows that you will not be overwhelmed.**

- Community involvement: **Employers love to see that you have done volunteer work. It shows that you take pride in your community, and a willingness to be a team player.**

- Company knowledge: **Again, this stipulates that employers like to see that you have done your research about their company. It shows that your interest in working for them is sincere.**

- Flexibility: **Employers want to know that you are able to go with the flow. It proves that they can depend on you later.**

- Ambition and Motivation: **Ambitious people are generally motivated enough to make great improvements in the company as they are working their way up the ladder. Ambition usually means more money for the company.**

- People skills: **Your ability to get along with others is very important to an employer. They need to know that you won't ruffle any feathers when you are hired.**

- Professional appearance: **Nobody wants a slob working in their office. Be certain to dress appropriately for the job that you are applying for.**

- Ability to Multitask: **This is getting to be a very necessary skill in the workplace. Most days, you will be required to multitask. Even if you are not, employers need to know that you can do it without freaking out on them.**

- Computer ease: **These days, just about every company in the world is running on computers. The ability to work a computer with at least minimal amount of ease is important. It is best to keep a leg up on the most common software like MS Office, Quark Express, and Linux.**

- Reliability: **Employers want dependable and reliable people to work for them. Your ability to arrive on time is a good place to start when trying to prove that you possess this quality.**

Employer Evaluations

Employers are generally monitoring and evaluating you on three skill sets during an interview. Those three skill sets can easily be broken down into these sections:

Content Skills

These are the skills that are directly related to performing a specific job in your profession. You get these skills by learning your craft in an accredited school through specialized training, work experience, attaining a degree, and internships. This shows an employer that you are have acquired all of the knowledge that you will need to perform your job efficiently.

If you do not have this type of skill available, you can simply express that you are looking into specialized training, and/or would be willing to start. It may not be exactly what the employer is looking for, but it shows that you show initiative.

Functional Skills

These are the skills that reflect your ability to work with others, and how you incorporate data. This is where an employer decides whether or not you are a team player. You can display this skill by displaying your past employment record and accomplishments that are directly job related.

Generally an employer will get an idea of your ability to work with others depending on your reasons for leaving previous jobs, whether or not your were fired before etc. If you have been fired before, don't lie about it, and do not act bitter about it when discussing the reason, this will not benefit you in the end. Be forthcoming and sincere. Express that it was a learning experience for you and tell them what you learned from it. It reflects well on your temperament.

Adaptive Skills

This is a general show of your personality and temperament. It also covers yourself management skills. During your interview, the employer will be evaluating you on your general ability to get along with him/her. Your general personality traits are monitored during this time.

When faced with a difficult question, you do not want to get defensive or angry. Just take a few seconds to think about what you should say rather than say something you will regret. If you must; simply explain that you are a little nervous so that you can buy a few extra seconds to answer.

You want to appear at ease, (or as much so as you can) during your interview. You want the employer to think that you anticipated everything that he/she is going to say. Even if you are terrified at your replies, do not let them see you sweat.

Summary

By now, you have learned everything that you need to know before you enter into an interview. During this manual, you have acquired the skills needed to get and ace any interview that you go on. You have made the right move in choosing this manual as your guide. As promised, you are going to approach your next interview with a leg up on the competition. By now, you have learned to:

- Get the interview of your dreams

- How to prepare for the interview

- The best way to behave during an interview

- How to make a great first impression

- How to build the best resume for your dream job

- How to create a winning cover letter

- What to do during a restaurant interview

- How to dress for success

- How to close an interview

- What question you will be asked during an interview

- What questions you should ask during an interview

- What questions cannot be asked during an interview

- How to follow up on your interview

- What employers are directly looking for from you

You have learned everything that you need to know in this guide, and probably a little more than that. Don't worry; if you have read and used all of the information in this manual, you have increased your chances of getting that job by 100%. If you are due to have an interview, you've already learned how to ace the interview just by reading this manual, so relax, and go get that job!